Scam!

A survivor's guide to cons and rip-offs

Steven Telfer

Illustrations by Abby Franklin
and Matt Windsor

CASSELL
ILLUSTRATED

First published in Great Britain in 2004 by Cassell Illustrated,
a division of Octopus Publishing Group Limited
2-4 Heron Quays, London E14 4JP

Edited by Elissa Telfer, Simon Myers and Michelle Pickering
Designed by Abby Franklin

ISBN 1 84403 2345
EAN 9781844032341

Printed in China

Contents

Introduction

It is human nature to remember bad things that happen to us. Of course we enjoy the good times, but it's the hair-raising experiences that we revive again and again over dinner with friends.

We deliver these stories with a light-hearted 'we survived' style hindsight, but at the time we'd all wish it wasn't happening. This is a book about things that have happened to others and myself, things that will always stick in our minds.

There are scams here that may have happened to you, some that you think you would never let happen, and others that… well, one day just might happen if you're not careful.

If you don't want to be a victim of scams, then this is the book for you. I hope that by reading it you'll be saved the anguish of finding that you're in the wrong place at the wrong time.

Travelling

Travelling the world can enrich your life, but with the good sometimes comes the bad. Cons, rip-offs and scams, all designed to take advantage of the unsuspecting traveller, are ever-present. From teenagers embarking on their first backpacking trip to seasoned travellers, all of us at some time will fall foul to a seemingly obvious scam.

The key to avoiding these clever deceits is in learning to recognise the telltale signs of the confidence trick before it gets fully underway so that you can sidestep a scam rather than fall prey to it. Following are some examples of scams you might encounter while travelling. Some are more prevalent in certain parts of the world, while others are just bizarre.

Train window

You're sitting on a train, waiting for it to leave the station. A person on the platform knocks on the window and loudly asks you for the destination of the train. You respond by shouting through the glass and making exaggerated hand gestures.

It takes you several moments to communicate the destination to the person who can't hear you clearly through the glass. Suddenly they nod and walk off. You sit back down and realise that your bags have disappeared.

Coat over the head

Short people look out. You are travelling on a busy bus or train but are lucky enough to have a seat. A man is standing near you, holding on to the rail with a coat over his arm.

As the bus goes over a bump, he accidentally drops the coat over your head. He helps you in your struggle to get it off and in the process takes your wallet at the same time.

Bogus pineapple

You are out on the town with friends, looking for a cheap place to eat. You see a pizzeria and, on closer inspection, notice a sign in the window advertising a cheap ham pizza special. Sounds perfect, so your small party piles into the restaurant and you each order the special. When the food arrives, you notice that the pizzas have pineapple on them as well as ham. You're hungry and can't be bothered to call the waiter, so you eat the pizza as it is.

When the bill arrives, you notice that the total is three times what you were expecting. You query the bill with the staff and are informed that ham and pineapple pizzas are three times the price of ham ones. As you have eaten them, the manager refuses to negotiate and insists that you pay the higher price.

VW trap door

VW Beetles are used as taxis in many parts of the world. The luggage compartment is in the front of the car and the front passenger seat has often been removed to allow more space to store suitcases. You hail one of these VW taxis and climb into the back seat. The driver packs your luggage in the front and you're on your way. On arrival at your destination, you pay the driver, thank him and check into your hotel.

Hours later you realise that your backpack has been rummaged through and your valuables taken. You are dumbfounded to think how this could have happened.

These VWs often have a hidden compartment under the front bonnet with a trap door. A small child travels in the compartment and, during the journey, opens the door and rifles through bags packed at the front undetected.

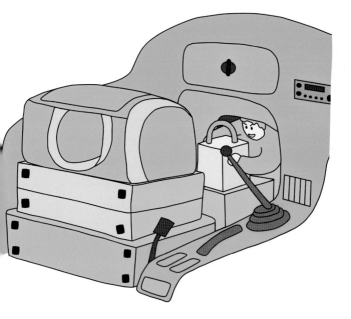

X-ray snatch

You're waiting in a queue to put your hand
luggage through the x-ray machine at the airport.
Your turn arrives and you place your luggage on
the conveyor belt to go through the machine.
Turning to walk through the metal detector, you
are surprised when someone abruptly cuts in
front of you and races ahead. In addition to their
queue jumping, they also manage to set off the
detector's alarm.

The guards instantly step forward and instruct
them to empty their pockets, which they do busily
while you wait with growing frustration. They
repeat the detection process a second time
without incident. You follow the person through
the machine and go to collect your bags from
the conveyor belt. You wait for a while before
realising they're not coming through. They've
already been taken.

You're in my photo

As a tourist in a new country you are keen to take lots of interesting photos.

You are sightseeing and are just about to take a picture of an old building when a local makes his way into your view. At first you think this is rather frustrating, but on second thoughts you think it could add some charm.

After you have taken the photo, they come up to you and demand money. Their generous act of standing in position has cost you.

Pants down

Women take their handbags everywhere and thieves know this. You are in a busy restaurant and go to the lavatory. You enter the ladies toilets and lock yourself in a cubicle. You put your handbag down by your side.

Someone enters the cubicle next to you and sits down. Suddenly a hand shoots out from under the adjacent cubicle and grabs your bag. You shout, leap up and open your door, but fall flat on your face with your pants around your ankles.

Foreign currency recount

On arrival abroad, you go to the bureau de change to convert your money into the local currency. The teller calculates the exchange rate, then counts out your foreign currency in front of you. She hands the money to you, you recount it and then she asks if she can count it once more just to double-check that it's correct. You agree.

Having counted the pile of notes already, you don't pay too much attention. She counts the money once again but this time slips some notes away for herself, then hands you a reduced amount. You walk away, not bothering to recheck it because you have already counted it once.

You gave me a fiver

This is a favourite trick used by taxi drivers when you're not familiar with the local currency. You are in a taxi, getting on very well with the driver; he's talkative and friendly. You arrive at your destination and the fare comes to just over £20 (or its equivalent in that country). The driver tells you not to worry and to make it a round twenty. You thank him and hand over a £20 note.

You busy yourself getting your luggage together, ready to leave the cab, when he interrupts and tells you that you've only given him £5. You apologise profusely for your mistake, he hands back the £5 note and you hand him a £20. He thanks you and you go on your way. Unwittingly, you've just paid £35 for a £20 journey.

Bags in the boot, Sir

Arriving at an airport, you head outside and hail a taxi. As you open the door of the cab, a friendly looking uniformed valet politely offers to take your bags and place them in the boot. You hand them over and climb in the back seat.

The valet closes the boot, bangs the top with his palm and off you go. You appreciate the service but are shocked when you arrive at your hotel and discover that one of your bags is missing. The driver claims he knows nothing about this very efficient valet service.

I'll post that for you

Unsuspecting tourists often fall prey to this common scam conducted by some post office clerks. You walk into a post office to post a bundle of postcards you've been writing to your friends and family back home.

A charming postal teller greets you and calculates how much the postage will cost. After you pay, they kindly offer to stick the stamps on for you and pop them in the outgoing mailbag. You accept their thoughtful offer, thank them for being helpful and go on your way.

Your friends never receive their postcards. Nothing really beats licking the stamps yourself.

Want to buy
a map?

You are sitting at an outdoor café with your wallet, camera or mobile phone on the table in front of you where you can see them. A man approaches you and asks if you'd like to buy his maps or postcards.

You decline, but he insists on showing you his merchandise and spreads them out on the table. You ignore him and are relieved when he finally leaves, only to find that, when he gathered up his postcards, your valuables left, too.

Someone stole my wallet

Sometimes a thief operating at a busy train station will announce in alarm that someone has stolen his wallet. Most people's natural reaction is to put their hand immediately on the pocket where they keep their wallet or purse to double-check that they haven't been a victim of the pickpocket as well.

Now the thief and his mates know exactly where everyone on the platform is keeping their money.

Taxi extortion

Disorientation is expected when you arrive at a new and unfamiliar airport. Con men are well aware of this and are often waiting to take advantage of you.

After passing through customs, sometimes you find yourself surrounded by scores of drivers touting for your 'taxi' business for the ride into town. One con starts after you negotiate a good price with one of the drivers (say, £20 for the ride to your hotel), then follow him to his unlicensed car and leave the airport.

Upon arrival at your destination, the driver insists that the fare is now £50, saying that the extra £30 is required for your excess luggage. A dispute arises but, when driver goes to get something out of the glove box, you notice that he has a handgun stored there. You decide to accept the new price and be on your way.

Carpet in the post

You're travelling through a country renowned
for the quality of its textiles and come across a
charming little carpet store. You decide to buy a
carpet and the shop owner asks if you'd like him
to post it home for you. He proudly shows you
his outbox of carpets, all wrapped, addressed and
ready for the courier to pick up that afternoon.

Not wanting the hassle of travelling with a carpet
slung over your back, you decide to accept his
offer. Some time later you arrive home, only to
find that your carpet has not turned up. It never
will — it was never sent.

Clean ears

In some parts of the world, 'ear cleaners' roam the beaches offering to clean the build-up of wax in your ears for you. Never having had this novel personal service before, you agree to a session.

The person pokes around inside your ear, then removes what seems like an incredible amount of gunk. Gratified at this unexpected clean-out, you hand over a princely sum – but it is for someone else's earwax.

What's your name?

When walking through a traditional marketplace, people often approach you and ask you to buy their wares and trinkets. Naturally, after a lot of hard sales talk, you feel relieved to talk to someone who doesn't seem to want to sell you anything.

You chat with the guy and talk about the town and the area. Eventually he asks your name. You tell him, thinking nothing of it. The man then proceeds to carve something into a small wooden object he has been holding. You look on, curious about what he is doing. Once finished, the man holds the carving up to your face and demands payment.

Carved into the wood is your name. You start to protest but the carver points out that the wooden statue cannot be sold to anyone else because it has your name on it. You have to buy it.

Hotel will pay the fare

It's the night before you're due to leave your hotel for an early flight from the airport. You arrange with the hotel's front desk for a taxi to collect you first thing in the morning. They tell you that in this country it's standard practice to pay them in advance. You assume that this is just a way for everyone to get their commission, so you agree.

The next morning you check out of the hotel, the cab arrives and you start your journey to the airport. Halfway there, the driver claims that the hotel hasn't paid him anything for the fare and you need to pay him. You argue your case vehemently · but he threatens to drop you at the side of the highway if you don't pay. Not wanting to miss your flight, you submit to paying for your ride a second time.

Misleading mileage

Some untrustworthy hire car companies have been known to fiddle with the odometers in their vehicles so that the mileage is more than you've actually travelled.

One way of fiddling the mileage is to put smaller wheels on the car than recommended by the manufacturer. If the rental fee is charged by the mile, they can increase their bill by up to 20 per cent without you actually driving any further.

Giant pigeon

It's a fine, sunny day and you are enjoying a walk through the town square. There is a tap on your shoulder, you turn around and a stranger points out a huge greyish streak of liquid running down the back of your coat. He points to one of the many pigeons on top of the local buildings.

You assume that the foul-looking mess on the back of your coat is indeed pigeon shit. You are annoyed and want to clean it up, but you don't have any tissues or water with which to do so. Luckily, the stranger does. You kindly accept his offer to help clean it off. He does what he can to fix you up, you thank him for his help and you both go on your way. Buoyed up by this friendly local gesture, you are shocked later when you discover that your wallet is missing.

Watch out next time. Ice cream mixed with cigarette ash, mustard or dirt squirted from a plastic bottle can look very like pigeon droppings.

Fill her up

Running low on fuel while abroad, you pull into a petrol station. A young man races out to attend to your fuel needs. Almost as soon as you've told him to 'fill her up', he has your petrol cap off and starts pumping. Unfortunately for you, the meter has not been reset from the previous sale.

Not bothering to check means that you end up paying double for the fuel. As if this is not enough, the attendant clicks the nozzle a few times to give the impression that the tank is full when it is not. It is only after you have left the station that you realise you have paid a lot of money for petrol that you don't have.

Money or your bags

This widespread distraction technique is often used in bus stations or airports where you are waiting with your luggage.

A man quietly strolls up beside you and, while you're not looking, artfully drops some money on the ground next to you. He taps you on the shoulder, looking very helpful, and informs you that you've dropped some cash.

Surprised, you thank him and bend down to pick it up. When you stand up again, your bags have gone from your trolley.

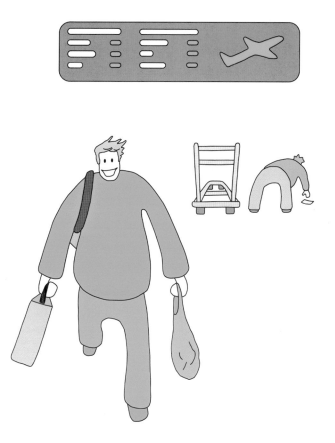

Jewellery swindle

You walk into a jewellery store and, while looking around at some of the affordable gems, you get talking to the manager. After chatting for a while, the conversation turns to your home country and to jewellery export. The owner explains that his country's laws only allows him to export a limited amount of jewellery before attracting high taxes, but as a tourist you can take out a large quantity without attracting any taxes.

The jeweller says he has a business partner in your home country. This partner can sell the jewels at three times the price he can get here and, if you'd like to take some jewels back home with you, he'll halve the proceeds of any sales his partner makes from them.

You think about this for a while. The store owner appears legitimate and the proposition sounds appealing. Another traveller enters the store and tells you that he has done this once already and is back for another trip. You could make several thousand pounds as a result of this easy transaction, so you decide to accept his offer.

Now all the store owner requires is a photocopy of your passport and credit card, and your address back home. He will also need you to 'purchase' the jewels via a signed imprint of your credit card to make everything legal and ensure that they are delivered to his associate. He claims that he will not process the transaction but will tear up the paperwork once the deal is complete.

You wait back at your hotel for the courier to deliver the gems but they never arrive and it's too late to stop the financial transaction.

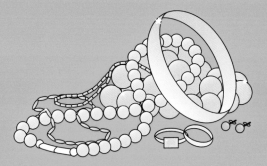

Drowning

You're relaxing and sunning yourself on a quiet beach when you suddenly hear the desperate calls for help of a girl floundering in deep water. Few people on the beach seem capable or willing to help her, so you run into the water and swim to her rescue.

Several minutes later (and quite exhausted), you return to the beach with the girl. She thanks you profusely and you head back to your towel. Arriving there, you find that your beach bag and wallet are missing.

At home

Your home is a place to relax, unwind and escape from the realities of life. However, with the advent of email, text messaging and the Internet, the home is becoming the ideal environment for criminals to take advantage of you.

Con artists can now gain access to large amounts of digital information about you, enabling them to target you personally in their scam campaigns. Once they're armed with this information, it's harder for you and legitimate businesses to recognise the con before it's well underway. Your best line of defence is to limit the personal information you release into the public domain.

Unpleasant reception

Having experienced difficulties with your TV reception you decide to call a TV repair engineer.

He arrives, climbs onto your roof and fiddles around. He comes down and tells you that in order to fix the problem you'll need a new aerial system; the other one is too old and will no longer work.

You reluctantly agree to the added expense but in reality the aerial had just been blown out of alignment and only required re-arrangement.

African millions

This is one of the most frequent and expensive scams. Amazingly, no matter how charlatan this seems, people are still taken in.

You are contacted by a person who appears to be from an official position Africa. A multi-millionaire client of theirs has passed away leaving them their fortune, but they need your help to access the money. You will be richly rewarded provided you tell no one about this. You are convinced that there is a real opportunity here.

Your contact needs a foreign bank account to transfer the money and while hesitant, you see no harm in providing your bank and contact details. Your new friend requires you to cover a catalogue of costs – taxes and administration fees so the money can be released – all of which you pay to get closer to your share of the money. Before you know it you've paid out thousands of pounds only to discover there was never really any hidden millions in the first place.

Apartment for let

Sometimes it pays not to tell everyone in town that you are going away for a long holiday. The day after you leave, an 'apartment for let' is advertised in the local paper. The scammers, knowing you are away, break into your flat and set up shop to receive a stream people responding to the ad.

Interested punters fill out application forms applying to let the apartment, while putting down a 10 per cent deposit to hold their claim on the property. The fraudsters accept a number of these deposits throughout the day, all the time issuing official-looking receipts.

When you get back from holiday, you find your flat is empty and you are confronted by an endless succession of angry apartment hunters wanting to know what is going on.

Job search
ID swipe

In the age of the Internet, more and more people
are going online to search for their dream job.
Unfortunately, gangsters are not far behind.
Some job advertisements posted on employment
websites are merely there to obtain your CV.

After submitting your details, you receive a phone
call informing you that a company is interested in
your application and requires more information
from you to run some 'standard' checks. This is
common for companies to do and, since you're
keen for the job, you oblige.

They ask for personal information and key details
about you, then ask you to supply a four-digit
'pass' number to access a work-related website.
Many people use the same numbers for
passwords as they do for bank PIN codes.
Several days later, you check your bank account
or receive a call from your credit card operator
informing you that your account is now in the red.

Make money typing from home

An ad in the local newspaper catches your eye: 'Use your computer to type and make money from home'. You have a computer and are a reasonable typist, so you decide to send away the required £20 to get your starter pack.

A few days later a parcel arrives for you in the post. Excited, you tear it open. Inside you find a computer disk and instructions. The instructions direct you to use the disk to make up ads to place in local newspapers asking people to send you £20 to 'Use your computer to type and make money from home'.

Don't call me

Receiving unsolicited phone calls at home from companies trying to sell you products or services is always annoying. When you receive a call from a telephone company asking if you'd like to be put on a DO NOT CALL register, you welcome the opportunity.

The person at the other end of the phone says that they'd be happy to put you on the register, but first they need to confirm that you are who you say you are. They ask you a series of personal questions, including credit card and bank details. You thank them for their help and hang up, pleased to be on the register. When you next check your bank account, however, there are thousands of pounds missing.

Fuse fire

A troublesome fuse at your home keeps tripping, so you phone an electrician to make a house call. The electrician arrives and examines the fuse box. You leave him for a moment, then return to be informed that the fuse box is faulty and for safety reasons needs to be replaced.

You wince at the thought of the expense but the electrician holds out a heavily blackened fuse that has short-circuited and started to burn, claiming that it could start a house fire if left unchecked. You're convinced by this argument and agree to the replacement.

In fact, the fuse box is fine. It was a faulty appliance that was the problem. The electrician has used a cigarette lighter to burn the fuse.

E-audit

You receive an email that claims to be from the
Inland Revenue. The email states that you've been
selected for a random electronic tax audit and
that you must complete and return an electronic
questionnaire within 48 hours or you will incur
mounting fines and interest. The questionnaire
asks for the usual personal and financial details
that are required on a tax return and you comply.

The next day you get a call from your bank, asking
why you have emptied your account.

Lost cat

Hearing a knock at your front door, you go to see who it is. A man handing out leaflets greets you. On the front of the leaflet is a photo of a cute cat whom he tells you has gone missing recently and he is trying to find her.

He's desperate to talk to anyone who may have seen her and says he knocked at the house next door but no one answered. He asks if you know whether your neighbours are away on holiday or if perhaps he should come back later in the day when they are home.

Through the veil of his heart-wrenching story, he is casing the neighbourhood trying to find houses that are easy to burgle while the occupants are away.

50 for £5

An ad placed in your local paper offers 50 cigarette lighters for £5. The offer seems too good to pass up, so you send a cheque to the advertised address and wait for your goods to arrive in the post.

A few days later a small parcel arrives. You open it and find a smaller than usual box of 50 cigarette lighters: a box of matches.

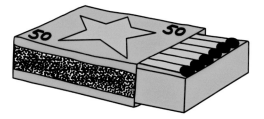

Modem switch

One Internet scam has web users greeted with a pop-up ad offering unlimited access to erotic material. All you need to do is download a free 'viewer' program to see the goods. You follow the instructions and, sure enough, you're supplied with a large selection of erotic pictures. What you're not told is that the 'viewer' you've just downloaded disconnects you from your normal Internet provider and reconnects you to another.

The program turns off your modem speaker, so you don't hear what's going on, and dials a new (often international) number. The new call is charged to your phone bill at exorbitant long-distance rates. When you leave the 'viewer' to do something else, the program continues to run and maintains the call connection. You may pay nothing for the entertainment but the telephone bill you receive at the end of the month will be enormous for you and very profitable for the scam operator.

In a box of 10

You receive a call from a woman claiming that her father's stationery store is moving to a new location. Stock is going cheap and you may like to buy some before the move. She quotes you specific prices for particular items, such as '£9.95 – in a box of 10'.

The supplies arrive, but when you get the invoice it is far higher than you expected. It turns out that the prices she quoted over the phone were per item, not per box as she implied. The box that you've ordered has cost you £99.50, not £9.95 as you expected.

Costly sandwich

You call a plumber to repair a leaking pipe in your bathroom. The plumber arrives and surveys the situation. He fiddles around under the sink for a while, then tells you that he needs a new part to fix the leak. A trip to the local hardware store will be required to see the problem right.

Two hours later he returns, fixes the leak and issues an exorbitant bill that includes the hours spent getting the part from the store.

Often the plumber has the necessary part in the van the whole time. In some cases tradesmen have been caught having lunch or napping while 'down at the store sourcing parts'.

Heavy breathing

You receive a phone call on your mobile but it stops ringing before you can answer it. You check the caller identification but don't recognise the number. You decide to call the number to see who was trying to reach you, but the call is answered by a recorded sex line. You hear some heavy breathing, dirty talking and the like and end the call. Although a little odd, you think nothing more of it.

Later in the month you check your mobile phone bill and, sure enough, the call you returned was charged at a high connection and per minute rate.

An automated process is used to make calls to lots of different mobile phones but cut short before they can be answered. Anyone who returns the call gets charged for the privilege.

Replacement part

Calling a tradesman to your home can be expensive enough without them trying to take you for a ride. An engineer arrives and studies your broken boiler. He pokes around for a while, then tells you he's found the problem but it will require a new part to fix it. Fortunately for you, he has a spare in his van. He takes the old part out to his van and returns a short while later with a box. He opens the box, pulls out the new part, unwraps it from the plastic and proceeds to repair your boiler. He charges you for the parts and labour and goes on his way.

It turns out that your boiler only had a small problem but, to increase his bill, he told you that it required an additional part. He took the old part out to his van, cleaned it up a bit, put it in a plastic bag, then inside a box and brought it back in. He put the old part back in your boiler and charged you for a new one.

In the neighbourhood

Most people have had the experience themselves or know someone else who has had their belongings targeted when at a local restaurant or club. However, losing your handbag or briefcase is just one of the many cons and rip-offs that could face you if you ever let your guard down when out and about in your home town.

The following scams range from credit card fraud to bizarre ways of relieving you of your belongings. Remember, thieves are constantly inventing new ways to take advantage of you, so staying alert is crucial for self-preservation.

Hot pants

Not everyone who wanders around with a large coffee in their hands wants to drink it. Walking through town, you have your hands full with shopping bags. A man walks past holding a cup of coffee. There's nothing out of the ordinary about this, but at the last minute he empties the coffee all over your trousers.

You scream out as the piping hot coffee burns you, drop your bags and instinctively start to brush off the coffee. At this moment the man grabs your bags and runs off.

Dropped change

This distraction technique is used on buses the world over. A woman stands up behind you and pulls the cord to get off at the next stop. When the bus slows down, she drops some change, a set of keys, her makeup or all three. Bits go everywhere and she begins climbing around trying to retrieve her belongings from under the seats.

Everyone stares at the woman with interest and confusion. While you're distracted, a young boy who is working with her swipes your bag and jumps off the bus.

Fortune teller

While walking along a street, you find yourself
confronted by a small group of gypsies. They tell
you that they want to read your palm. You try to
turn down the offer but one of the women grabs
your hands and begins the reading. She tells you
a delightful story of meeting a tall, handsome
stranger and having lots of kids, all the time
holding your palms firmly.

The other women crowd around, looking
on closely with interest, but when the crowd
disperses you find that she left out the prediction
that you'd have your pocket picked in the very
near future.

Escalator fumble

You're riding up an escalator in a shopping centre when the woman in front of you drops a packet of cigarettes just as you're approaching the top. She fumbles around for her cigarette pack, blocking your way while more and more people start to pile up behind you. Some people bump into you. Someone says sorry. Just as things get difficult, the woman picks up her cigarettes, apologises for any inconvenience and wanders off.

You continue with your shopping but, when you reach for the wallet in your back pocket to pay for lunch, it's no longer there. Then you remember being 'bumped' from behind while on the escalator.

71

Plastic sleeve

It's Friday night and you go to a cash machine to make a withdrawal. You insert the card as usual and enter your PIN. To your surprise, the cash machine bleeps a 'card invalid' error at you and retains your card. A bystander comes up and asks what the problem is, which you explain. They suggest that you try your PIN again, which you do to no avail. The machine appears to have swallowed your card and you'll have to visit the bank the next business day to retrieve it. You walk off frustrated.

When you visit the bank to get your card, you discover that it is not in the machine and your account has been emptied. A crook placed a small plastic sleeve into the card slot just before you arrived at the machine. The sleeve stops the cash machine from reading your card and leads you to believe it's been swallowed. In fact, the card is just stuck in the plastic sleeve. The helpful stranger later removed the plastic sleeve (also known as a Lebanese Loop) with your card in it and emptied your account.

Damsel in distress

This scam plays on a natural masculine sense of chivalry. Walking down the street you suddenly notice a man snatch a young lady's purse. As he makes a run for it the lady screams for help looking in your direction for some assistance.

You feel obliged to run after the thief who is weaving in and out of the crowd ahead. Racing around a bend you find yourself in a dark alley face to face with the bag snatcher, and his gang of friends. You get mugged, the young lady's (empty) wallet is returned to her by the assailants and the scam starts all over again.

Handbag on the hook

This sophisticated bag theft takes place in the ladies lavatory. After entering a toilet cubicle and closing the door, you hang your handbag on a hook on the back of the door and turn around to check the seat before using the toilet. When you turn back, you discover that your bag has vanished.

Racing frantically out of the cubicle, you see a woman standing at a basin. She tells you that she saw the thief bolt out the door. You follow quickly in hot pursuit, only to find when you get outside that the bandit has evaded you.

What happened was that the woman was watching your feet under the cubicle door. She sees you turn away from the door, then leans over the top to grab your bag. She quickly places your handbag inside a larger carrier bag, then misdirects you out the restroom to chase a phantom bag snatcher.

Police pull over

Driving along a road, you are waved down by two men standing next to a car. They're wearing what look like uniforms and they signal you to pull over using an official-looking torch. The men request to see your licence, saying they are on an operation to find an escaped prisoner, and ask you where you are going. They take away your licence for a few minutes and one of them seems to check it back in their car. They return it to you, thanking you for your cooperation.

Relieved, you return home, only to find that your house has been burgled. While you were waiting for the 'police' to return your licence, one of them phoned their associates, who broke into your home knowing exactly how long you would be away.

Share the find

You are walking down the street one day when you see a wallet on the ground. Before you can get to it, a man arrives and picks it up before you. You both look at the wallet and notice cash and credit cards inside. Your collaborator suggests that the owner will never come back and it would be fair to split the cash between the two of you.

The idea appeals and he recommends that the prize be shared away from prying eyes. You both make your way to a quiet back street where, to your surprise, your new friend has a change of heart. He decides to keep the wallet and now takes anything you have as well.

Flying hairball?

You are driving along a busy street when the traffic lights ahead turn red and you slow to a halt. It's a warm day and you have the windows down. The pavement is busy with people shopping, eating and chatting.

Suddenly from out of the crowd you see a small boy run towards you and hurl what looks like a large ball of wet brown fluff through your back window. While obviously concerned, you don't think it's anything serious until suddenly the ball of fluff begins to move and you realise that it's a rat.

As the terrified animal scampers around the floor of the car, you open the door and leap out as fast as you can. While you stare in shock at the car, thieves run out from the crowd, jump in and drive off.

A21 TNV

Phoney heist

You walk into a bank to withdraw some money from your account. As usual, you fill out the withdrawal slip and take it to the counter. The teller goes about her business, processing your transaction until suddenly the blood drains from her face. She glances at you with great unease and begins to remove large wads of money from the cash drawer and place them on the counter. You look on with wonder at the increasing mountain of banknotes.

Suddenly, you are grabbed from behind by security men, pushed to the floor and handcuffed. Someone with a bad sense of humour has written 'This is a hold-up, hand over all your money' on the back of the withdrawal slip.

Guaranteed for life

Have you ever tried to take a set of tools back
that have a lifetime guarantee? You go to the
store where you bought a spanner that is now
broken. It came with a lifetime guarantee, so you
cannot believe it when the store owner refuses to
replace the broken item or refund any money.

He claims the agreement is only guaranteed for
the lifetime of the tools, not your lifetime. Since
the spanner is now broken, the lifetime of the
tool has clearly ended and so has the guarantee.

Bill from the copier company

While working in an office you receive a call from a man. 'Hi, it's Bill here from the copier company. Would you confirm the model number of your photocopier for me?' He sounds friendly and familiar, almost as if he's been dealing with your company for years. Not knowing any better or thinking there's anything odd about it, you give him the information. He thanks you and hangs up.

A couple of days later some boxes arrive addressed to you. You open them to find out what's inside and discover that they're filled with copier toner and an invoice. The courier company refuses to accept the goods for return because you've opened them and the copier company insists that you pay.

Cigarette and the watch

You're driving your car through the city and get caught in a traffic jam. It's a hot day; your window is down and your watch arm is resting on the car door. A young boy runs through the immobile traffic, grabs your arm and, before you know what's happening, he slips off your watch and runs away.

Next time you go out, you have wised up and wear your watch on your other wrist. The boy has also smartened up. This time he runs through the traffic, burns your window hand with a lit cigarette and, as you reach over to stop him, he grabs your other hand, slips off your watch and runs off.

Is this your money?

While withdrawing money from a cash machine, someone taps you on the shoulder and asks if you've dropped a £5 note, pointing to one on the ground.

You bend down to pick it up, then stand up to find that your card has gone from the machine.

Pretend dialling

You're standing in a queue at a department store, waiting to pay for some goods. The queue moves slowly but it's getting there. In one hand you have a pile of clothes and in the other your wallet and credit card, ready to pay the cashier. You notice a woman in the queue behind you dialling someone on her mobile phone. You don't take any notice because people call each other from everywhere these days. The queue moves forward, you pay for your goods and leave.

A few weeks later you get your credit card statement through the post and find several transactions on it that you never made. You've not let your card out of your sight for a moment, so you cannot conceive how anyone was able to use it without your knowledge. How on earth did these transactions happen? Then you remember the woman behind you in the queue dialling.

Spot the pea

You're walking down the street and come across a game of 'spot the pea' using three matchboxes. You watch for a while, noticing a man playing and betting but never guessing which matchbox has the pea under it. The location of the pea seems obvious to you, and the guy operating the boxes seems pretty useless.

The player invites you to join him, offering to go halves in the bet and share the winnings. You feel super confident and decide to join in but are soon losing a lot of money. The men are professionally inept.

Crash test dummies

While driving at night, you break to stop at some traffic lights. The car behind you breaks late and hits the back of your car, slightly denting your rear bumper.

A bit shaken, you get out and walk around the back to assess the damage. One of the men in the car behind also gets out, but instead of helping with the accident jumps into the driver's seat and drives off with your car.

Blurred vision

People who wear glasses, look out. Walking through a busy retail area carrying your shopping bags, you are intent on getting home and unloading your recent purchases. Suddenly, a man walks straight up to you and spits in your face and all over your glasses. Just as quickly, he runs off.

You can't see a thing. Stunned, you stop. Putting down your bags, you pull out your handkerchief and take off your glasses to clean them. It's at this moment, while you can't see very much, that another man races out from behind you, grabs your bags and sprints off through the crowd. Putting your glasses back on, you discover that all your shopping is gone.

Lucky flower

A couple of gypsies approach you offering a good luck flower. Before you have a chance to reject the offer, one of them pins it to your lapel. She says all you need to do in return is give her a penny for luck. You know you don't have one, but she insists that she won't accept anything more than that.

Reluctantly, you get out your wallet and start looking through it. She offers to help search for the coin, and, while she pokes through your change, she shields your view of your wallet, grabs any cash she can get, thanks you and walks off.

Credit card swipe

You ask for the bill after finishing a meal in a restaurant. The waiter comes over, collects your credit card from the table and takes it to the till for processing. You notice that he takes a while to return.

A month later you receive your account statement and thousands of pounds are missing. Under the shirt of the waiter was a small electronic swipe device used to skim credit cards and store the numbers. These numbers are sold to others to create a cloned copy of your credit card.

Hold my baby

You're sitting on a park bench one day when a man holding a baby approaches you. He looks a little stressed and asks if you can help him for two minutes by holding his baby. He tells you that he has to run back to his car to put some more money in the meter before he gets a ticket from a parking warden. You agree reluctantly. He thanks you profusely, hands over the baby and walks off quickly around the corner.

Moments later a woman runs crying into the scene. She sees you with the baby and races up to you screaming. She yells at you, claiming that you've kidnapped her baby. A jogger appears as well, claiming he also saw you steal the baby. They threaten to call the police unless you return the baby and pay them to keep quiet.